ANIMALIAN

ALSO BY NORAH POLLARD

Leaning In
Report from the Banana Hospital
Death & Rapture in the Animal Kingdom
In Deep
Lizard Season

ANIMALIAN

Poems by
Norah Pollard

Antrim House
Bloomfield, Connecticut

Copyright © 2021 by Norah Pollard

Except for short selections reprinted for purposes of
book review, all reproduction rights are reserved.
Requests for permission to replicate should
be addressed to the publisher.

Library of Congress Control Number: 2021905251

ISBN: 978-1-943826-82-7

First Edition, 2021

Printed & bound by Ingram Content Group

Book design by Rennie McQuilkin

Front cover artwork by the author

Author photograph by George Magdon

Antrim House
860.217.0023
AntrimHouseBooks@gmail.com
www.AntrimHouseBooks.com
400 Seabury Dr., #5196, Bloomfield, CT 06002

*In memory of my mother, Agnes Conlon Pollard
and my father, John "Red" Pollard.*

And in memory of my brother, John Michael Pollard.

We were the "potty Pollards."

Acknowledgments

I wish to thank my son, Matthew Christianson, for the expert technical help he provided during the making of this book, without which I would have hanged myself.

And I am so grateful to my daughter, Nicole Dionis, who encourages my efforts by pointing out that, though I was a "C" student in high school, I now can count (poetic feet) and spell (mostly).

Thank you, my loving children, for raising me.

Table of Contents

I. My Town

St. Mary's By The Sea / 5
Diogenes' Son / 6
His Majesty, Man / 8
The 97 Percent / 10
From a Tower, One Cannot Know the Earth / 12
All Praise / 14
Mirth / 16
A Garden Scene / 17
The Collector's Apologia / 19
Damp / 21
No Bones About It / 22
Habits / 24
The Sadness of the Nonstarters / 26
The Angel and The Lion / 29
Edna Gopnik / 32
A Calling / 35

II. Reflections & Speculations

An Alleluia / 39
A Moral Enquiry / 41
The Question / 43
Help! We Need Somebody! / 45
Against Optimism / 46
Why I Go To The River At Night / 47

III. I Am I

Loneliness, the Yellow-Headed Bird, and Me / 51
How to Save Yourself—A Self-Help Poem / 53

Anthem / 55
Animalian / 57
His Name / 59
Grief / 61
I Have A Longing / 63
You Think I'm Good / 65
Mourning the Wild World and All Created Things / 67
I Compare Myself To A Happy Woman I Know / 69
Inheritance / 71
The Jewel in My Father's Crown / 73
The Mailman And His Trees / 75
Shame 1 / 77
Shame 2 / 79
Dragons On The Line / 81
Wet / 82
Need / 83
I Am I / 85

IV. The Men

#YouToo / 89
The Power of Dreams / 90
A Single Man / 92
Id Est / 93
One Man's Meat / 95
Soldiering On / 96
Mal / 98
Stratford Morning / 100

V. How you say…?

One Of Those Days / 103
Hinky Dinky Parlez Vous / 104
Very Small And All Good / 105
Death, You Bitch / 106

The Tunnel / 108
Pen & Ink / 109
The Elderly Thought Fox / 111

VI. Colors

In Florida / 115

About the Author / 121
About the Book / 122

Keep a green tree in your heart and perhaps the singing bird will come.   – Chinese proverb

ANIMALIAN

I. MY TOWN

St. Mary's by the Sea

At St. Mary's By The Sea,
the big sailboats, big skies, big houses
look out over Long Island Sound.
The Sound's waters slip into estuaries
that form deep pools near the shore.
In those summer pools, wading through cordgrass
and sea moss, the Portuguese women from Bridgeport
drag wide nets between them,
catching herring fingerlings and the occasional eel.
The women's skirts are hitched up to their waists.
They chatter and laugh. They sing.

When a net is full, the children following their mothers
bring up the buckets and the women fill them
with hundreds of steely-blue fish.
The women laugh, the children laugh.
It even seems the sun is laughing.

Some people strolling to the Black Rock Yacht Club,
some walking their groomed poodles along the esplanade,
and some, looking down from the windows of the big houses,
wonder what the Portuguese ladies have to laugh about.

But some, seeing the laughing women and children,
think back to when they were young
and remember when they laughed like that,
and are wistful.

Diogenes' Son

This winter a young man moved into
a broken-down house in my neighborhood.
He began fixing it up.
When, on one of my walks,
I stopped to pet his cat,
we met.
We immediately began to talk about
the deep things. A surprise!
Who talks like that? No weather, no recipes,
no ball teams, no Aunt Edith's hip replacement.
It was a delight.
He quoted Yeats and Spinoza.
He quoted Churchill in Churchill's voice,
"…we shall fight on the beaches…,"
with even more fury than Churchill.
He said his house had no heat yet,
but he was fine with his one electric heater
in the room with the bed.

We met again on another, colder day.
We talked again of deep things.
He invited me in and I went.
It was even colder inside.
There was nothing to sit on.
There were planks and ladders
and saws and screwdrivers
and that's all.
I wondered how he would survive the winter.
I didn't ask.

We stood in the cold kitchen that freezing day
while he quoted Roosevelt, Malcolm X,
Oprah, Kennedy and Michael Jordan.
He wondered if John Wilkes Booth was a good actor.
He quoted Cromwell and then Woolsey.
He conversed in quotes.
He was terribly earnest.

And when he asked,
"Do you believe there is Truth?"
so fervently did he ask,
so desperately, his eyes so intense,
his face so close,
a slight quiver in the word "Truth,"
that I sensed a craziness in him,
a holiness, a tilt.
When I said goodbye, I knew
I would not be back.

This winter has been long and bitter.
I wonder from time to time
how he's surviving.
I wish he'd come to my door and say he's cold.
I wish I'd bring food to him.
I wish I had courage.
I wish I weren't afraid of a man so mad, so rare
as to search for Truth.

His Majesty, Man

The river floods a few times a year.
Police and firemen drive through town
bellowing into bullhorns,
"River rising, river rising!
Move to higher ground!"
The flood sirens wail.

But no one ever leaves.
We watch the river rise,
we watch as it oozes through the seagrass,
slides over the road, creeps up the bluff.
We were warned. But we wait and watch.

I've seen the river in bad storms—
I've seen the river's middle bulge,
churning up swells big as ocean waves
tossing boulders around,
pitching boats up in trees,
grinding the roads to salt.
Each time the first responders wailed their sirens,
hollering, "Take evacuation routes!"
We were warned.
But we watched and we waited.

The river has always subsided. So far.
Gone back to its bed like a weary kraken.
But someday the river will take us.
The wind will howl, the sirens will scream.
We'll have been warned.

For now, though, we'll still watch and we'll wait
because it is innate that we believe ourselves immortal.
Too, there's something in us needs to face a wildness,
something in us needs our complaisant lives disturbed.
But our greatest need is to feel
we've won out over Nature.
So that when the flood recedes,
we can feel we've been brave,
we'll have stories to tell,
heroes to claim—accidental or invented—
and hubris to spare.

The 97 Percent

The 63-year-old secretary on her lunch hour
took a "Town & Country" magazine
from the doctor's office.
That is to say, she stole it.
Rolled it lengthwise, pressed it under
her armpit vertically, and left unseen.
People don't notice much.

She had told the doctor that the pain in her shoulder
was worse when she mowed the lawn.
The doctor said the words "rotator cuff" and told her
she should hire someone to mow the lawn.
That other pain in her forearm, that was carpal tunnel.
He could operate, he said.
She should get another job, he said,
one that does not involve typing.

Secretaries type. She was 63. What could she do at 63?
And secretaries cannot pay $40 an hour for a gardener.
She didn't tell the doctor any of that.
She thanked him. She lied when she said she'd consider
the surgery—the surgery she knew she couldn't afford.
And then she stole his magazine.

That night she took two aspirins with a glass
of Rolling Rock and turned the pages
of "Town & Country." She looked at the pictures
of women and men so beautiful and perfect
they were boring. "Oh, for the love of God,"
she spat, "show me a hooked nose!
Give me one crooked tooth!"

She looked at pictures of a $38,500 David Webb ring,
a Louis Vuitton handbag for $2,050,
a Tiffany necklace for $26,000.
Some items were listed "Price on request."
The price too shocking to print, she first assumed,
and then remembered the old saying, "If you have to ask...."
That's "Town & Country" for you, she thought,
and took another swig of Rolling Rock.
But what she wanted to know was,
    Whose town?
    What country?

From a Tower, One Cannot Know the Earth

One night Texas sent us remnants of a hurricane.
The wind shrieked, old trees came down,
the ocean drummed and drummed—
the whole world making din like an orchestra gone mad.
The next day, when calm had come, some friends and I
made a trip to Misquamicut to see the waves
and what the storm dragged in.
A fellow came along, a visitor, a friend of a friend.
I knew only that he was a Greek and Latin scholar,
a professor from the city, a brilliant mind.

At the ocean, the sun flashed and flared on
great blue walls of water two times higher than our heads.
The massive breakers, convulsing at the peak, plunged down
to smash the beach—the ground shook like tremors from a quake.
The waves looked like great steel harvesters coming for us.
They sounded like a million mortars homing in.
We were in that state between ecstasy and terror,
that happy-fright a rollercoaster gives a child.
Electrified, thrilled, we stood and faced
the massive rollers rolling in.

But the professor turned back. Rigid, white,
he cried out in panic, "No!" And then he ran.
We found him crouched behind the sandbreak,
shaking and shaking while he held his head.
We were reluctant to leave the ocean,
that gorgeous spectacle of *son et lumiere,*
but he was so distraught.
We took him home.

He left straightway, back to the city university.
(He later wrote, I heard, a lauded text on Alcibiades.)
I've thought of the professor from time to time—
not with the mild contempt I had at first, but with some pity.
He was just a man whose life lacked a physical footing,
a man who lived in his learned mind. He probably dreamed
in ancient languages of Latin and of Greek.
He saw the gorgeous, formidable world as from a tower,
and he feared
because he did not know the language of the earth.

All Praise

A woman makes a hat and wears it.
Someone says, "What a hat! What a pretty hat!
You could be a hatter!"
And the maker of the hat smiles.
She thinks that over.
She decides to make a few more hats.
Then a few more after that.
She makes herself into a milliner.
Somewhat well-known, too.

Near Grand Central, a boy dances to hip-hop
for coins. Two women watching say,
"What a dancer!" And, "He could dance with Alvin Ailey!"
The boy hears. He turns up the rap and
pours even more wildness into his breaking.
He's filled with fire and desire.
He begins to think of schools and scholarships.
He decides to dance for his life.

And a man in a cubicle steals time
to doodle a horse and rider.
He's observed by a co-worker who says,
"Man! You could be an artist!"
The doodler, for the first time,
takes his doodling seriously,
goes out and buys some paints,
becomes a painter.
He paints himself right into the galleries.

Those millions of other folk
who cherish a talent but live their lives

like seeds locked under rocks,
stillborn, delivered into nothing
for lack of the validating word—
those other millions?
They die dreaming.

So praise the singer, praise the song,
praise the actor, weaver, cook,
praise the boy into a man,
praise, all praise to all you can.

Mirth

The world tickled my father.
He had a talent for laughter.
He laughed at the just and at the unjust.
He was not crazy.
He was not cruel, never cruel.
To the friend who broke his toe,
the friend who got arrested for drunk driving,
the friend who got nailed for doping his horse,
the friend who had the blues because his woman ran out,
my father would say: "It could have been worse.
It could have been *me*."
And then he would laugh and snort and hoot,
and his laughter was so gleeful and innocent and wicked,
we'd all get to laughing because
when my father laughed, nobody could help but laugh too.
And the owner of the tragic tale, especially the owner,
would laugh, and his laughter and dad's laughter
and our own laughter would keep on
until we were weak with it,
the tears dribbling down our faces.
And the laughing owner of the tragic tale
was magically cured of his melancholy—
at least for a time.
Then, spent, we'd all sit around grinning,
limp and calm, each of us silently allowing
how absurd life is.
None of us blaming anyone.

A Garden Scene

I read aloud the little stringed tag on the teabag:
      "If you give happiness,
        you will get happiness in return."
"Oh," the thin lady said, "let me video you
reading that! It's so beautiful!"
"No," I said.
The thin lady's smile went away.
Our hostess asked, "Why not?"
"Because I don't believe it," I said.

I saw I had disappointed them.
I even felt they might be thinking
I had mocked them.
I felt guilt, for I had cast a pall.
I tried to explain to the two ladies
that you can give happiness—and often—
and not be graced in return. Often.
But they looked as if I were instructing them
in something immoral.

We were having tea under the arbor.
The sun glittered through the grape leaves,
plump jays in the garden whooping and
screaming like fat ladies on a game show,
bees whispering among the poppies.
This was happiness to me.
You don't get it only because you give it.
It's there, all around.

Then our hostess's husband came by laughing
and rubbing a clutch of purple plums on his shirt.

They were glistening from having just been washed.
He presented a plum to each of us.
The hostess said to her husband,
"Did you wash these, John? Have they
been washed?" Like a scold.
"Yup," John answered.
"Are you *sure?*"
He looked away.

So I commented on the artist-lady's necklace—
a stunning thing she said she'd bought in Rome.
"How much did it cost?" asked the hostess.
She did not wait for an answer, but turned to her husband,
"Why are you still standing there?
Why don't you mow the lawn or something?"
He looked away.

He had brought us his laughter and
those purple happinesses.
But she was not happy,
and he did not get happiness back.

The Collector's Apologia

He likes things.
He would like to have things that mean something,
things that were given him by someone he cares about,
or things that he found or collected at some meaningful time—
say, when he was with someone he cared about.
But not many meaningful things like that
were given him in this life. Not many.
Not enough.

Probably no one has enough given to them.
Probably most people accept this.
Or perhaps they don't mark the absence
in the first place.
But he is driven to make it up to himself
for the things he feels he needs
that no one has given him.
So he buys, takes, collects, palms things
that have no meaning at all…
except in being the thing itself.

Now he's old and finds himself
surrounded with gorgeous clutter.
It's all, of course, a substitute for love.
No mystery there.
He thinks on all the folks who love and are loved,
those who have been given things by their beloveds.
He expects that when their loved ones die,
their meaningful things will mean even more,
will be gilded with meaning,
and the *meaning* will be the meaning.

Whereas, he has and will always have the thing itself,
the pure, the simple thing, unburdened by
any moving recollection or sorrowful memory…
or meaning.
Just the beautiful thing—the Randall knife,
the Homer watercolor, the girandole clock,
the Victorian pocket watch…
Das ding an sich.
And things will always last longer than love.

Damp

A cold, wet spring.
The lawn has turned marshy.
Dead worms garnish the sidewalks.
Unsinging birds.
The peonies and rhododendrons
bloom for only a day before
being shredded by a cutting rain.
The fields are watery
and the river has drowned the road.

Inside, the ceiling is peeling petals
of plaster that float slowly down.
All the books are poxed with mildew.
The wallpaper curls at the seams.
You can't sweep—the dirt just smears.
Moss has measled the cellar walls,
and there's a stink in the air like
ancient excrement.

Water.
Fish swim free and clear and clean in it.
This is not that.
This is breathing dark cloud,
tasting invisible mud.
This is when men's brains and souls
are so sodden, so chilled,
only hell or lust can warm them.

No Bones About It

The soft-mouthed cat brought in the mouse.
Alive.
A little skirl of smoke, it evanesced
behind the bookcase.
Well.
The cat had caught the mouse in the great outdoors.
He would catch it in the house.
Surely.

Months went by. I saw no remnants
of a mouse. But one day
the refrigerator began to make a noise
like all the slot machines in Vegas.
A din.
With crowbar and pliers, I pried the fridge's
back off. Inside, wrapped around the condenser fan,
a mouse nest of napkin shreds, plastic bags, elastics,
string, and piles of fine black seedy poop.
Piles.

It takes some kind of mettle to overcome disgust.
I am short on mettle.
But I gloved my hands, I held my nose,
I gagged, I persevered.
I cleaned the whole mess out.
Entirely.

To Home Depot for mouse traps.
In the mouse trap aisle, I told my story
(how we love to tell our stories)

to the orange-aproned Depot lady.
I should not have.
Not.

She grew admonitory, prescriptatory,
she eyed me with a hint of scorn.
"You ought to know that mice can get in anywhere,"
she reproached. Then added,
"Mice have no bones."
None.

I smiled. I said, "Well, they have *some* bones."
Her eyes grew squinty. She leaned in
close as a dentist, breathed her heat on me.
Perhaps the clearing of her throat
only sounded like a growl.
And then she pounced—"No bones!"
"Most animals…" I began.
"Mice have no bones," her voice
colder, clearer, very much less kinder,
the voice of certitude—obdurate and fierce.
I sensed ferocity behind that orange apron.
I did not argue further.
No, not me.

It's strange what people will believe.
It's strange what people live and die for.
How keep the peace, how love, how teach
when there are those who will believe
their comforter and savior is the Reverend Jim Jones,
the moon is cheese no astronaut has ever walked on,
Elvis is alive and well, and
all mice have no bones.
No bones.

Habits

Freud smoked 20 cigars a day.

She smiles from the time she gets up
to ten minutes after she falls asleep.
Is her smile all unconscious—a porpoise smile?
Is she simply happy?
Or is she tense and can't relax her face?
But it appears, as she confided to me once,
she started practicing her smile (achingly) all day
because it lifted her jowls, made her look younger.
And now it's habit.

And why does he take the pencil,
always in his left shirt pocket,
to tap and tap on his knee?
He must do this. It's habit.
Never without the pencil,
or if not the pencil,
a coffee stirrer, a lobster pick,
a straight twig, a spoon.
Tap, tap, tap. Since he was ten.

I knew a woman who would steal things.
It was reflexive, it was automatic. A bad habit.
She'd see a thing small enough to pocket,
and she'd take it—a crystal egg,
a cut-glass salt shaker, a silver ring.
Anything that sparkled compelled her to palm it.
She'd put these sparklers in little boxes
and hide these in yet bigger boxes in the barn.

So many boxes! Once acquired,
she'd never look at those sparkly things again.

My cousin clears and clears
her throat for no good reason.
There's nothing there. It's habit.
The sound she makes every five, six sentences
is that of snow shovel on pavement.
One fears she'll shred her larynx.
She is, by the way, forever cleaning house—
a bit of OCD, I'd say.
She must be clearing clutter from her craw.

I have a friend who'd been in prison
(prison = bars around routine) who,
since his release, will always say,
"Routine. You need to make routines your habit.
Follow the rules and walk the line."
This may keep him sane and out of trouble,
but now my felon friend can never do
one spontaneous thing.
Nor does he know he carries—it's just his habit—
a prison on his back for all his life.

We are less free than we think.
We're often hobbled by our habits,
bound by our routines.
Yet a habit can be the thing that holds a man together,
simple as a string holds a string bean to a pole.
Every one of us has habits.
Freud cannot tell us why.

The Sadness of The Nonstarters

"I am in mourning for my life."
– Masha, in Chekhov's "The Seagull"

Two women I know—
we'll call them Maisie and Louise—
are in constant mourning
for their lives. They have been so
since I have known them—
and it's been a long, long time.
They feel they've not "done something"
with their lives.
And they have not.

Maisie's mother is to blame.
Maisie says she could have been an actress—
she was in a play in college.
She could have been a dancer—
she was top at tap at Hattie's School of Dance.
She could have played tennis with the pros—
her parents paid for lessons
at the Longwood Cricket Club.
But her mother, oh her obtuse mother!
did not think to encourage her,
thus her talents were stillborn—
so Maisie mourns.

Louise does not know who she is, she says,
and blames her having, long ago,
three babies in a row.
The babes, now in their 50's,
don't know her either.

She says she'd like to be a writer
and write about her life,
but she never reads a book
to find out how it's done
(nor does she have a life).
She says she'd like to paint a portrait,
but she cannot think of whom.
Louise regrets what she's not been,
though she confesses she does not know
what it is she could have been,
or what she wanted to become.
And that's a problem.

Neither Maisie nor Louise make an effort
at any kind of art,
though art is what they feel is in them,
and art it is which would redeem them.
So they cry, "I could have been…,"
thus becoming more adept at succeeding
to feel less-than.

I tell Maisie one needs a talent and the drive
to get where one would wish to be.
Without these, you must accept
you're one of every-other-fish in the sea,
of which most are relaxed and happy…
which it is o.k. to be.

And to Louise I say, the world has need
for pedestrian fish as well as Bluefin Tuna
or Russian Sturgeon roe-to-go.
But Louise continues to insist,
"I am no ordinary Joe."

Alas, for Maisie and Louise,
you can't convince them of any of that,
for they are special, they're unique,
although they cannot tell what at.

"I coulda' been somebody," said Marlon
on the waterfront.
Amen to that, and furthermore,
Dumbo could have been a swan
were he not so fat.

The Angel and the Lion

On a crossroads near my home is a grassy rotary,
a tiny local flea fair where unwanted things
are dumped and everything is free.
Today, a wooden rocker, a box of shoes,
two half-dead potted palms, and
standing in the center, white and glorious,
is a winged and stalwart angel.
And a lion.

How were they ever brought here? And from where?
Some cemetery nearby, perhaps,
or the lion from the courthouse
and the angel from the sky.

I cross to the little island to touch them.
I feel I am in some deMille Bible scene.
The angel, oh, she's gorgeous! As tall as I am,
outspread wings with individuated feathers—
and each feather has an edge.
The only thing amiss—she lacks a head.
But I'm glad she's headless.
Headless makes her noble—she's been through the wars.
Too, now I can envision the head of anyone I like
resting on her shoulders—
Jane Eyre, Ruth Bader Ginsberg, Norah Jones.
No banana curls or simpering smile. No halo.
And even though she has those two flat breasts,
I could imagine her a male…say, Gabriel.
I touch her. Cold and slick, this winged marble woman.
I'm in love with her. I want to bring her home.

And the lion! Large as a real one!
All white stone, lichened green between his toes and ears.
He's an old and lordly lion.
His mouth is firm and kind, not fierce, not snarling.
His eyes are blank, as though he's seen enough.
His tail—a miracle it's not been broken—
extends straight out horizontally
giving him the look he's on the move.
Oh Lion, walk you home with me!
I love you, too. I want to bring you home.

But how would I get them home?
A derrick would be needed.
And how would they fit in with
my white-cottaged neighborhood—
so predictable, so tidy.
Scandalous! A lion and an angel
on my Vine Street postage-stamp front lawn!

My neighbors would first be shocked to laughter
at the old and crazy lady on the block.
Then immediately they'd get up a petition
(Outrageous! The angel's tits right there!)
to have the salacious angel carried off.
As for the lion, he would have to be eliminated,
for he would frighten the neighborhood children
who must be sheltered from imagination at all cost.

I rub my angel's back and stroke my lion.
Though I cannot bring them home,
I'm hopeful no one else can either.
I'll visit on my walks, and when I do, I'll pray,

"Oh, Guardian Angel, oh Lion of Judah, save us!"
For we all need deliverance from mediocrity,
and preservation from wooden, conventional souls.

Edna Gopnik

Edna Gopnik was older than our high school lot.
And she was—the only way to say it—
ugly.
Short, stout, and vaguely misshapen,
hair like weathered rope,
enormous teeth and every-which-way,
and there was about her an odor
of things unpleasant.
No one taunted her. We merely avoided her—
a biological aversion.

From time to time after graduation,
I'd think of Edna and wish that I'd been kind.
I'd also wish I'd known her story.
Edna could be a novel, she was that strange.

Amazingly, in my junior year of college,
I ran into Edna in the cafeteria.
I was astonished to see she'd made it into college.
She looked the same. She was the same.
This was my chance to make amends, I thought,
…and a chance to learn her story.
I spoke to her and she,
so glad to see me, so grateful,
invited me to dinner.
And I went.

The college was in a rural town.
Her home was in the woods nearby—
two chickens running free in

a shack with a dirt floor,
plastic sheeting on the windows,
and tacked on all the inside walls were
unframed pictures of Jesus.
In every spare space, a crucifix.
An older woman, skin the color of mushrooms,
served up a stew I was afraid of.
All through supper Edna chattered about Jesus
as though he lived just down the road.
Sometimes she'd address him, as if
he were there in the room.
The old woman was mostly mute, but sometimes
she'd murmur, "Say it. Say it," or "Say the word."
When the meal had ended, Edna asked me
to go with them that night to a Christian meeting.
And I went.

I went with them, though no Christian,
to a barn even further in the woods
where twenty-or-so people prayed
and sang and swayed.
At the end, the minister called for all to stand
who would give their life to Jesus.
Edna stood. She smiled down at me.
There was a radiance about her.
She offered her hand, entreating me,
and I took it.
I stood. It was a lie. But for me,
kindness always trumps honesty.

After that, whenever I saw Edna
I would wave. But I avoided her.
Again.

There was that old guilt,
but I'd counsel myself:
How can you love everybody?

Five years later I saw Edna Gopnik's name
in the obituaries of the college journal.
I felt a kind of dim dismay
for her short, shunned life.
I stood still, remembering Edna
talking with her Jesus.
And then came the cold recognition
that I never really wanted to know Edna.
I only wanted—like a reporter
sniffing for a story—
to know her facts.
And I stood ashamed.

A Calling

For Brooke

It's graduation day for the kindergarteners.
A teacher directs a small group to sing a song
about a white and a black mouse.
(We are careful about racism here.)
Another group then drums on coffee cans. (Awful.)
Next, a troupe of red-wigged kids do a shuffling dance,
banging into one another,
going in wrong directions,
forgetting what to do.
(I think how flawlessly Chinese children
would have danced.)
One child stands still looking grimly down
like someone looking through the gates of hell.
And now they're all being given balloons.
Two little boys fight right down to the floor
because one got the color the other wanted.
The coveted balloon pops. The boys howl.

Order restored, finally comes the finale.
The kindergarteners stand on a makeshift stage to answer,
one by one, the principal's ridiculous question:
"What do you want to be when you grow up?"
Ralphie or John or Sam says, "I want to be a fireman."
We clap.
Jeannie or Debbie or Naiomi says "I'm going to be a nurse."
We clap.
Several say, obsequiously enough,
    "I want to be a teacher."
And on.

At last, the last little girl takes the stage and prissily recites,
"I want to be a doctor…"

We clap
We clap extra hard because finally,
finally, this whole shivoo is over.

Except…
though the teacher is waving to her from the wings,
making shooing motions and hissing something,
the little girl continues to stand, looking gravely out at us,
motionless and silent.
The teacher claps her hands, she you-hoos,
she snaps her fingers. She's angry-while-smiling.
Finally the graduate, chin up in slight defiance,
takes one step forward and declares to all, "And also,
I'm going to be a mermaid."

We clap and clap.
We clap long, we clap loud, some even whistle
because, we all understand, this is the child
who will be a poet.

II. REFLECTIONS & SPECULATIONS

An Alleluia

For Rennie

The world is frozen.
An ice storm all day long.
The black cat runs out,
a black *glass* cat runs in
all iced over.
By late afternoon, every wisteria vine,
clothes line, willow switch and weed blade
is fixed in ice-glazed rigor.

My old maple tree has been dying
for a few years now.
The arborist who came out told me
nothing could save it. "But," he said
to console me, "it will take some time to die."
Since then, a spring wind will take a branch,
a heavy snow amputates several.
Still, the tree holds on.
This fall, instead of flaming into crimson,
its leaves turned the grey-white of old folks' skin.
In December now, stranger still,
not one leaf has fallen.
They hold on.

Tonight the wind picks up.
From the lip of each iced-over leaf
sways a small spike of icicle.
The whole tree, lit by streetlamp,
glints and flares.

As the winds increase,
I watch the tree's spine shudder, its branches throb.
The tree shakes out light like an aspergillum.
All night the leaves clack and rattle—
the death breath.

This morning I open my door
and there stands the old maple glistening in the sun,
radiance haloing it like an Alleluia.
No rebirth for the old tree, not a resurrection,
just the more earthly triumph of abidance,
the victory of holding on
miracle enough.

A Moral Enquiry

On the vast asphalt parking lot,
the seagulls brood on their situation.
They stand shoulder to shoulder, a colony
of at least one-hundred,
all facing in the direction of the east wind.
The white lake of feathers is aswim with black spies' eyes—
gulls sighting like wartime snipers for some food.
Here comes a man from Subway, next to Walmart,
eating something in a big roll of bread.
When he's finished, he casts his crusts on the blacktop.
Immediately the gulls, through twenty yards away,
interpret his pitch and fly up very fast very high.
The flock soars tight, like a single sheet flapping from a clothesline.
They fill the air with screeching… awful!…
like a choir of Ku Klux Klaners singing "The Magnificat."
A quarter of the gulls fall upon the bread—
they fight each other like murderers for a crumb.

Looking up at the cumulous of white, blue-bottomed birds,
beautiful in their orbiting and white sway,
one feels blessed, uplifted, as if one glimpsed a frame of heaven.
But if one looks to the gulls waging violent war on the ground,
one sees a frightful scene of hell.

Standing in the vast black parking lot of Walmart's world,
like watching from a peak in Darien,
one looks and looks and does not know how to view it.
Making it anthropomorphically/philosophically/teleologically personal,
would one rather fly hungry in heaven,

or practice viciousness, but be fed, upon the ground?
It's hard to know.
The bread is gone,
the seagulls silent upon the lot in Walmart land.

The Question

We go around and around,
we go to and fro,
our cranias a cosmos of memories,
beliefs, plans.
All of us alone.
No one really knowing the whole of another.
No one really knowing the whole of oneself.
We walk up and down.
The kind and the cruel walking around
as well as those that are neither.

The great human herd covers all the earth,
living, dying into others' memories,
then those others dying.
And the human herd keeps going
like all herds—munching,
rutting, walking up and down on the earth.

Animals are more spiritual than Man.
They have grace to sense what they were made for
and they do it.
No ulterior motives.
No fretting about their circumstances.
They live and don't ask why.

But to every human in the human herd,
the question eventually presents itself:

>   But what is the purpose?
>   What is the meaning?

And the question—for which we have no answer—
will ever after rattle in our skulls.

Oh, we'll still strut to and fro
and we'll still swagger up and down,
      but in disquietude, and at uncertain pace.

Help! We Need Somebody!

In the old days, God admitted to dumping floods,
sending locusts and plagues, sulfur and fire,
and persecuting poor old Job.
God was irritated, wanted to prove a point.
Maybe just having fun.
We'd pray, "Help us! Save us, Lord!"
And when the torture ran its course,
we'd praise him, thank him, cook him up
braised sacrificial lamb.

Now, though, he doesn't talk to us anymore.
Well, he's very old. It's probably dementia.
Still we pray and light candles.
Sing his praises La-La-La.
We say, "God doesn't give us more
than we can bear."
(And the suicides pile up
and the sad go mad.)
We say, "Everything happens for a reason."
(God alone knows what it is, but He's not sayin'.)

Asking God the All-Powerful for help
when he could stop the sins against humanity
to begin with, is humiliating.
Crawling and crying is humiliating.
We should know better.
But we are so needy, and not everybody loves us,
so we hang on to the Imaginary Friend in our head
because it's better, it's oh so better
than nada, zero, nihil, zilch
when you're suffering or dead.

Against Optimism

The dolphins are in the doldrums,
The whales strand on the shoals.
The gill-net chokes the gull,
The crabs rend sea-drowned souls.

The different are hated,
The destitute have-nots cry,
The children are slowly starving,
The wars, they multiply.

The lark's on the wing, you say?
The sun is in the sky?
All's right with the world, you say?
      You lie.

Why I Go to the River at Night

The river's long black tongue
takes the snowflakes like communion.
I watch.
I grow colder and freer.
I wait.
I watch and wait until all my little ideas,
obsessions, complexities, my hatreds
as well as all my loves
melt away like the snow on the river.

This is the reason I come to the river at night.

The sky grows blacker, the snow whiter.
In the dark near the rocks, a white mass
is floating towards the pilings.
A small iceberg?
Hard to make out.
Now the mass has become muzzy forms
shaped like question marks.
It comes to me that the night, the snow, and the river
are being asked a question.
I'm thinking on this when—

Swans!
Two white swans, question and answer both,
enduring in the dark,
swimming into all that white.

Night annuls and night brings forth.
There is always something to find in the darkness
if you put yourself there.

III. I AM I

Loneliness, the Yellow-Headed Bird, and Me

Most poets admit to it.
It is a favorite topic.
I am moved by their loneliness
if they're eloquent about it.
They help me to imagine what loneliness is.

Maybe you'll think it's a prideful stoicism in me,
or a kind of arrogance that
I prefer my own company to others.
But I tell you, I am never lonely.

Alone, yes.
Yet I don't nurse a vodka at the kitchen table at dusk
remembering the special good old days.
There weren't any.
Or thinking of a man who used to love me.
There wasn't any.
I'm not weeping in the dark
missing the companionship of my kind.
I've never met my kind.

And so I don't miss anything
to make me feel lonely for it.
Loneliness is merely the atmosphere of my life.
It is simple, like the air.
I breathe it, like the air.
And, like air, it is not something you can describe,
or have a feeling about.
In fact, like air, loneliness can be something you need.

There is a bird that has come to my yard this spring.
It appears to have no mate.
It's a bird I've not seen before—
brown and white with a yellow head.
No other birds fly with it.
Still, it sings and sings from dawn
until the North Star's rising.

How To Save Yourself – A Self-Help Poem

As students in Dr. Leone's high school French class,
we were not allowed to look left or right,
not allowed to slump, not allowed to ask a question…
unless we knew the answer.
We could only look down at our book,
the scarred desk, our hands,
or up at old Dr. Leone's crimped tin-tinted face.
It was a torment.

But one day I found that I could twist my ring
towards the window so all outside was mirrored
on the ring's stone table.
I could look down at my ring and see in miniature
sparrows, clouds, airplanes, dragonflies—
all bathed in the blue-green-purple
of the ring's Alexandrite stone.
All during class I'd watch the captured sky
like an astronomer.
And so it was I was saved from a terrible boredom
and the mollusk mug of Dr. Leone.

I failed French.
But what I did learn was how important it is
to find ways to escape into the beautiful.
We search for the beautiful. It is instinctive.
When death comes to your old dog,
before you lay him in the hole,
you linger to see, to feel, and so to remember
the beauty of his silver coat.
You notice the gorgeous shades of copper on the

scales of the corn snake... before you run.
You are struck by the luminous porcelain
of your mother's skin as she reads by the window.
It is a comfort to you to watch how gracefully
the willow's branches sway in the wind.

Beauty is the palliative, beauty is the opiate,
beauty is the remedy for the world's harshness.
Beauty is all around us for the beholding,
or, if not,
you must imagine it.

Anthem

The summer before my first year of college
I worked at the Royal Electric Company.
Each morning a rack of wires taller than my head
would be wheeled up to my soldering station.
I'd spit on the safety goggles, pull on the canvas apron,
tin the tip of my iron, melt the solder under the
copper wires, fuse them to the two brass plugs…
and smell and taste pennies all day long.
When I was done soldering the 1000 cords to
the 1000 plugs, another rack would be rolled in.

Each workplace was lit, but beyond these small lights,
the plant was in twilight.
In this gloom, at noon,
I'd sit with other aproned workers
on metal benches lined up beside the rest rooms.
Not much talk among them, and they didn't talk to me.
The miasma of smells in the plant—chemicals,
burning rubber, melting plastic, tint of old sweat—
kept me on the fringe of nausea.
I never could eat the sandwich.

The real torment was the PA system.
It's deafening buzzer would shock us
to start, to lunch, and to leave.
All the time between, the PA blared
"The Chipmunk Song" eight hours a day,
day after day, all summer long.
The "chipmunks" sang in screechy,
teeth-on-edge voices conjured by the

varying of tape speeds.
The cutesy Christmas song irritated the meninges
and twisted the brain—it was a kind of pithing.
It's purpose, I assumed, was to
keep us all working in 3/4 time.

None of us went whistling down the road
those summer days at five.
We'd line up, punch out and walk out into the sun
stunned, aged, stooped, sapped.
After work, I would be too tired to meet with friends,
of whom I had grown resentful anyway.
They did not know what work was.

In the fall, I entered college
and stepped into another life.
It was as if I'd awoken from a brutish sleep.
Light everywhere! Light!
I read the poets, studied French,
learned about Thermopylae.
By two weeks, the smell of the plant had left my senses.

But even as I read about the Inuits and the Dinkas,
as I dissected frogs and labeled moths,
as the teacher intoned Keats' glorious words,
I still could hear the chipmunks trilling in my brain—
though now they voiced what came to be
the anthem for my life:
"You are lucky, lucky, lucky, lucky!"
was what the chipmunks sang.

Animalian

The lioness, the vixen, the polar bear, the yak
all have four teats.
The camel, the buffalo, the dog, and the lynx—
they have four teats.
Me, I have the usual two in front—
round, pink, hairless, happy-to-meet-you breasts.
But tucked under each armpit
like secret treats, like survival snacks,
like sweet confections in the hoarder's larder,
are podgy corporeal pouches
small as coin purses—
nipples for clasps.

I was twelve when I noticed them.
What were these strange lumps?
A deformity, that's what.
I told no one. I became alien and ashamed.
I never again stretched my arms out to the sun,
or wore a sleeveless shirt or bathing suit,
or went to girlfriends' sleepovers.
I kept my fleshy secrets hid,
like sins.

In my twenties, I fell in love.
He loved me.
He kissed me everywhere.
He found my secrets
and he kissed those, too.
When our child was born,
my atavistic, supernumerary breasts

filled with milk.
"Unusual!" said the nurse.
"Rare!" said the doctor.
My babe suckled in turns
at my four rich wellsprings
while I lowed and purred and hummed
to my pupple, my kit, my little lambkin,
my famished foal.

His Name

"Creep" was our laughing nickname
for each other into middle age.
Initiated when we were teenagers—
at first a name-calling but soon
a calling-name—having no meaning to us
but brother, sister, ally, friend.
Creep was our name.
A short word, Creep. A satisfying K click,
the R soft and growly, the EEP sound
a young pigeon hawk makes.
Creep.
An old joke. A signal. A greeting. A *name*.

When my brother lay dying,
the nurse, tapping gently on his cheek,
kept calling out "John"—his never-used
given first name—trying to awaken him for me.
And the name I called him, leaning over him
trying to sing him back,
was what our parents called him.
Michael! I called. Michael!

I felt to call him Creep would have been
interpreted by the nurse as a meanness.
Not a polite thing, Creep, to call a dying man.
And I have been polite—suicidally polite—
all my life.
Our name for each other seemed suddenly…
embarrassing.
So I did not summon my brother with our special name,

even while I knew in my heart
if he heard me call "Creep,"
he might waken, or might, at least,
have sensed I came,
I was with him,
I was there.

What's in politeness and etiquette?
   Punctilios. Tea with old ladies.
   Diplomats over vodka. Pretense.
   Fictions and flatteries.
   Veneer over truth.
What's in a name?
   Everything.

Grief

I don't weep.
Is my heart so hardened?
Maybe I am stoic.
Maybe I lack the lacrimal glands.
Or how about conditioning?
Who cried at home when I was young
and much to cry about?
No one.

There was one time I almost wept.
After the tour in a cold basement room
full of caskets, after choosing
the lilac-lined one for our mother,
we drove in silence to a drugstore
where my brother bought his cigarettes
and I bought cheap silver earrings…
I don't know what for.
Next we went to a coffee shop
to sit among the normal
to feel normal.
My brother smoked his cigarette.
I sat numb. I drank my coffee.

And then it came, the stunning pain
—physical and real—
a shiv in my heart,
a cud of thorns in my throat,
the weight of a glacier on my chest.
I could not breathe.
I gripped the table and stared down,

hearing nothing,
seeing nothing.
Grief wrung me like a rat.

A minute passed in stillness.
The coffee cooled.
The coffin dimmed.
The pain subsided.
I had not cried.

I have known grief.
Known it and known it.
Kept it. Harbored it.
Grief does not escape from me in tears.
It seeps deep into my body
where it grows its crystals in the darkness there,
hard, sharp, incorruptible—to last a lifetime.

Deep night is when grief comes,
keen and crystalline, to cut the heart
and pierce the eye that sees afresh the losses lost,
but will not cry.

I Have a Longing

I have a longing now to know horses.
Why did I not know earlier
that I wanted to know them?
I buy a pottery horse
at the Dollar Store.
Made in China.
Three inches tall.
White. The hooves white, too.
Black around the eyes.
Black mane and tail.
Is the splash of lemon-yellow across its flanks
a mistake?
Perhaps it's far-east sunlight.
I have a white horse.
A horse with white hoofs.

I grew up in a town.
Then I moved to other towns.
And now I am in the town I'm in,
and there are no horses.

Where are the horses?
Out on the Southern Plains.
I would have to move there
to know the horses.
Look for horses in Kiowan country.
Come to know the Kiowas,
the finest horsemen in the world.
They would teach me to know horses.

But I am too old.
They say it's never too late.
But truthfully, for most things,
by the time you wish you'd done something
you didn't do when you were young,
it's too late.

I live in a town.
I have a white-hoofed horse.
But it does not breathe.
It cannot run.

You Think I'm Good

I am not good.
When I am dead, you will say,
"She was a good woman."
You will say you knew me well.
"She had the gift of intimacy," you'll say,
thinking you were my confidant.
I'll lie there in that wood and satin box
and you will kiss my cheek or touch my hand.
You might even weep.
"She was so kind," you'll say.
I am not kind.

I have secrets. I have a secret life.
What I am is socially adept— that is to say,
I know how to act in the world.
How to be.
And I can read you. I know what you want.
I know how to compliment and comfort.
How to entertain at tea.
But inwardly,
I have a secret life,
and it is not good.

I am not good, but I prefer it.
Good can be banal and tedious.
Good has little imagination—
just follow the rules.

My greed, addictions, my critic's eye—
all this I hide behind my mild regard.

I smile, I listen, I incline my head,
I might even hold you close to me.
But I am not good.
I'll never tell you why.

Mourning the Wild World and All Created Things

When I think of death, my own death,
I am not sad for the loss of my self.
That is not imaginable, in any case.
But what I think of, and already mourn,
is the loss of the things that sustain me in this life,
the material things that excite my interest,
incubate my pleasure, keep me in the hold of joy.

Milkweedy clouds, giant trees,
east-sweeping winds, the long green river—
these are not my body's flesh.
But they are what compose my spirit
and what my spirit composes.
When I die, they die.

And it will be all my many material things—
the great jade plant that fills the window,
the watercolor of Yolanda on my wall,
the classic beauty of the French mantle clock—
golden Diana and her golden dogs flanking its face—
it will be all the things that furnish my spirit,
these tangible *things,* that will die
when I die.

Were I to believe in heaven, I would not like it.
I prefer earthly things to permanent bliss.
Bliss is a passive thing, a thing best experienced
with closed eyes and emptied mind—like death.

It will not be the loss of self I regret—

its hungry ego, talents, morals,
indiscretions, needs.
It is that the world will die to me when I die.
And I will continue to the end to mourn—
for mourning is a kind of love—
the inevitable loss of this world's
strange and lovesome things.

I Compare Myself to a Happy Woman I Know

She loves to chatter.
She believes adamantly
in untrue or dead ideas.
She walks around with a head
full of falsities.
It is so heavy with certitude and pride
her lids do not open all the way.
She has a spasmodic high-C laugh.
She laughs because she is happy
because she knows what she knows.
She has a talent for faith.

I have a flair for doubt.
Nothing is ever certain.
Change reigns.
The earth shifts, the light wavers,
rivers change course,
there is no God,
there is a God,
life is a comedy,
life is an agony,
death is to be avoided,
death is a blessed relief.

The happy woman is so certain.
I am not so certain.
Curiosity is my religion.
A low-voltage expectancy
keeps me on the *qui vive*.
My days hold surprises.

Wonder keeps me unsteady
on my feet and in my head—
like being dizzy from dancing
or laughing too hard.
This is so much better
than mere happiness.

I think.

Inheritance

When Dorathy, my ex-husband's mother, died,
I went to her wake.
We had always remained strong friends.
No *ex* applied to us.

In the receiving line,
in the hush of the flower-sated room,
the ex I hadn't seen for 21 years
snarled for all to hear,
"Stay away! Stay away!"
It was a scene.

He feared, I think, that I would comfort his father.
(As I knew he would not.)
Or perhaps he thought I wanted her things.
Man's reasonings are dark.

A granddaughter inherited Dorathy's wedding ring.
Another was given her mink.
Today, a package for me.
Folded and wrapped in newspaper,
Dorathy's underwear.
An old woman's frayed, not-quite-white
rayon stuff—you could not call it lingerie—
elastics stretched, lace limp, stitches unraveled.
She would have felt so embarrassed.
For *her* I feel shame.

From the worn items in the box,
these last, basic essentials of hers,

I pull out a too-small camisole
and tug and wrench it over my ribs.
She draws her scent around me.
She holds me hard.

The Jewel in My Father's Crown

was his glass eye—iris the deepest sapphire,
jet pupil, milk glass sclera.
For many years I've wished that
before we'd buried him, I'd asked the mortician
to give me my father's eye. Secretly.
(The family would not be pleased.)
I would have carried it home and placed it on a swatch of silk
high on the the bookcase shelf, looking down, vigilant,
watching me go about living my life,
watching me grow old.
We would speak with our eyes, my father and I.
I would ask his advice, tell him of my good day,
whisper of my sorrows.
He would be with me.

I had never spoken of this longing.
Friends would find it macabre, perverted.
Incestuous, even.
Family would think, Shame.
But yesterday at the library, when I asked the librarian
how she hurt her eye—she had a patch—
she said a prosthetic eye was being made for her.
In a sudden ditching of reserve, I confessed
how I longed to have my father's blue eye.
"Yes," she nodded, "and do you know? I still keep
my father's artificial leg."
We looked into one another.
"It's just…" she said, "it's only we want to hold on
to them. To something of them. Something intimate."

We laughed together briefly.
No.
No, it wasn't laughter. More the kind of
soft nickering sound humans make
when they understand each other.

The Mailman and His Trees

for Gary

I think continually of the mailman.
It's odd, I know. Some kind of quirk.
It's not that I ever expect him
to bring me a special letter.
Just that I am attuned to him.
He comes to my mailbox each morning.
The lid clanks like a fired blank.
No special letter. A bill, maybe.
An ad for pizza.
He'll also pick up an outgoing letter of mine
jammed like a white flag of hope
—or surrender—
between the planks of my house
and the nailed-on mailbox.

In the afternoon, I'll see him two streets over
walking under the trees,
leafing through an armful of mail.
Or I'll see him parked at the entrance
to the burned-down theater
eating his lunch under the great sycamores
in his little square truck,
so red, white, blue and true.

I'll see him carrying a package
to the pretentious house on Elm
guarded by those silly cement lions.
I wonder what he thinks of those lions.
I see him in his blue-grey uniform

carrying all those silent words on heavy paper,
the weight of his mailbag growing lighter
and lighter as his working day draws to a close.
At the end of it, he must feel so light, so light
he can fly!

Am I romanticizing? Am I forgetting the rain
and sleet, the snow and the damn gloom?
Yes, I suppose.
It's just that I'm envious. Yes, that's it.
Every day he gets to walk under the trees,
in silence, alone,
his knees regular as pistons,
his legs steady-going as a paddleboat,
his mind thinking all sorts of things,
or maybe in a kind of meditative trance.

All my working life as a secretary—
sitting, sitting, sitting,
typing other people's thoughts, taking dictation
from other people's heads, answering phones
for other people, writing down messages
from people for other people,
and sitting until my hind is deadened,
my shoes smell like onion,
and the owls in my head are begging for trees…

how I longed to have a window,
a little window I could look out
to see the trees.
Wishing I could walk under their auspices
in sacred silence all day long
like the mailman.

Shame 1

Every day, every hour, the Housatonic
is a different river.
HIGH TIDE—whitecaps all across to Nell's Island.
MIDDLE TIDE—water a black oily liquid full of
strange swimming forms way out.
(They may be seals. Sometimes they are.
Mostly they are water forms,
sculptures the current heaves up to tease the imagination.)
LOW TIDE—large cobbles emerge from the water's edge
like heads wearing wigs of seaweed.

In winter, I can be alone at the dock with the river.
But warmer days bring out the men.
Big men with slack bodies, slack mouths.
Men who drink from brown bags and curse.
They rage. They laugh. They punch.
They play their car radios—
a dissonance of different stations so loud
you cannot hear the river's rustlings.
They dump their car ashtrays on the sand,
throw their beer cans in the river,
puke in the reeds.
They'll spit on your shoes.

One late afternoon, the sun plating the waves,
I watched these remnant men throw rocks
at the gulls and mallards.
No, I thought. These men do not love.
I went up to them and said,
"Stop throwing rocks at the ducks."

Said it plain, like that.
I did not say please.
I was afraid.
They called me Bitch, but they did stop.
At least while I was there.

But last spring, mid-March—
the herons just returning, the swans
circling slowly—
one docker began to hoot and shout
that they all should shoot a swan
and eat for a week.
The others took up the cry.

I was weak.
Afraid of guns, feeling hopeless,
I did not speak up to those pigs,
but turned toward home along Shore Road.
The great blue sky and its blooming clouds
could not comfort me.
The delicate water reeds could not comfort me.
Not even the great river itself could comfort me,
nor the red-winged who kept calling from the marsh,
"Take heart! Take heart! Take heart!"
      For I had not any.

Shame 2

A summer's night.
A thin white fog on the river
like a sheet on a bed.
Smell of weed and low tide.
The men are fishing.
Loud music from two car radios'
different stations create a mood
of things on edge.
The men fish and drink.
They throw their beer cans in the river.
They're getting rowdy.
Catching fish is not their goal.
Getting drunk is their goal.

Parked next to the dock, an old blue Chevy
with the trunk open. In the trunk
is a little girl around seven or eight.
She's sobbing, crying, "Uncle Jim,
Uncle Jim!" over and over
as three men, drunk, laughing, clowning,
push her down and in and slam the trunk.
Hopping around, punching each other,
hooting and laughing, now they open the trunk
saying, "Come on out, scaredy cat, come on now!"
When she scrambles to get out,
they push her back into that black hole
slamming the trunk again. And again.
And again.

I am there.

I watch.
There are men around who could help the girl,
men not so drunk as Uncle Jim and his friends.
They do not help her.
Jim and his friends are drunk and crazy—
the kind of drunk that can turn murderous.
I stand very still near the black rocks.
I am afraid.
I back away.
I turn and cut through the field for home.

~ ~ ~ ~ ~ ~ ~

I'll always think of that child and her terror.
She'll be grown now.
Is it possible she's happy?
Or in her heart does she know
help will never come.
There is no help.

I like to think, since that night,
I've shown more courage in my life.
I think how courage can come and go.
Can be in you one day and not another,
depending on mood, weather, energy,
time of day.
I think how you can live with a shame
lodged in the back of your brain like a bullet,
festering there your whole life.

Some things you cannot forgive yourself for.
And you should not.

Dragons on the Line

The clothesline stretches between the garage
and the old locust tree.
The clothespins clamped on it these some years
are blanched grey, a part of nature now.

Every summer come the dragonflies
to swarm and cluster on the line
among the wooden pegs.
Like bits of stained glass,
panes of the dragons' veined wings
glint gold and green in the sun.
Their enormous eyes take in the world.

At times the dragonflies will lift at once
to drift and dart awhile among the peonies
before settling again along the line
between the clothespins.

My clothesline is a Mecca the dragonflies
make pilgrimage to each year.
Perhaps, to dragons' eyes, the clothespins
look to be their mummified ancestors.
Perhaps they take their ease among
the weathered pegs the way I'll stop awhile
amid a graveyard's crop of crosses
for the sense of homecoming.

Wet

Rain   rain   rain
for days until I go insane
and on this third day
rise up and run out in it,
dodging thunderclaps and lightning,
sticking out my tongue to taste.
(Rain tastes like rain.)
And then I slosh and stomp
through lake-y puddles
(becoming seriously wet).

But—strange!— my lunacy is turning
somehow joyous.
I feel like an evangelical being christened,
an immigrant whose visa's been authorized,
a poet receiving a literary prize.
I whoop and howl in the murderous gale,
I whirl in the roar.
I feel exuberant and arrogant
and I holler at the sky,
"I refuse to die!"

It's just now I see
a blazing lightning bolt has met
and murdered the weeping willow tree,
and quickly add to my defiant declaration,
"At least, not yet."

Need

You can't always get what you want
But if you try sometimes you just might find
You get what you need.
              – Mick Jagger, Keith Richards

We were young—my husband and our two friends—
when we took the early ferry *Uncatena*
to Martha's Vineyard on that holiday.
It was the water I was looking forward to—
something I rarely saw back then.
I was so happy to imagine I'd be on deck
to see the face of water, its silver-blues and greens,
to sense its depths.
But the other three were smokers
and the wind was up.
They stayed inside the cabin and they smoked.
So I stayed inside as well.

The smoke was thick. It was a scrim
that did not let that summer's morning in.
Conversation, like the smoke, was thin.
Through grimy portholes, I stole glances at the sun
and the seagulls skirling in the sky above the stern.
How I longed to leave that haze of smoke,
step outside and lean against the railing,
to smell the spray and watch the water churn
and scud against the hull.
To see horizon.
But I stayed inside.

I stayed inside, despite my fiercest longing,

because I thought to leave the three
might seem discourteous, impolite,
at the least, unfriendly.
(I had been brought up to be courteous and pleasing,
had been taught it was rude to let my wants be known.)

On Martha's Vineyard we walked on cobblestone streets
past small shops packed with seashell jewelry,
anchor keychains, mermaid paperweights.
We had a hotdog lunch somewhere I can't remember,
then walked till dark on the Vineyard's cobbled ground.
When we left to go back on the ferry,
the water was a blackness. That was all.

To have forfeited the water's green-glistening flow and foam
seems too small a matter to have caused in me,
for all these years, such sorrow and self-blame.
Unreasonable that I would mourn a mere disappointment
as keenly as if I'd lost a lover or a home.

But the water had something to do with freedom,
a right I did not allow myself back then.
Had I—selfishly, unmannerly, without leave—
freed myself that day to be with water,
I'd have known then how to recognize, claim, and treasure
the things I need that keep my soul alive and free.

I Am I

I am torn between the hormone and the halo.
I am split between the spirit and the real.

I ride the winds of ecstasy and sorrow.
I love the lovely, yet foul draws me as well.

My soul: a field of negative/positive energy.
My person: a duality of openness and guile.

I am I.

I see both sides and can't choose either one—
for truth is mixed, and nothing—as well as all—is a lie.

In shadowed corners I whisper my confessions.
I shout my theories to the blue unsounded sky.

I'm of nine minds, open to every possibility.
I accept them all, and so my Being thrives.

IV. THE MEN

#YouToo

Oh, the hard-hatted men
with the soft-hearted grins,
they'd whistle when I'd sashay by.
Yes, yes, when the dark-eyed man at the party
smiled and gave me the eye.
And yes to the lips and the loins and the hips,
and yes to the stroking and rising.
And yes, oh yes to the feeling desired—
it kept me gay and going.
I danced and danced to the songs of sin,
and sang my sutra, "Tits to the sun!"

Now I am old—as you too will grow old—
undesired except for my wit.
And now I know I will never again
be touched by libidinous men.
It is a loss, it is a great loss, it makes you terribly blue
to lose the beauty and strength and lust of your body,
and your breasts droop down to your shoe.
They'll tell you wisdom makes up for this.

Not true!

The Power of Dreams

Sudhir Singh Gupta, the copper-skinned
man from India, never smiled,
walked about like a subedar major.
He was a sultan of consultancy,
the maharaja of merchantry,
brought in to shape up the company
and make it more profitable.
He could see and ferret out
every problem, every lack of economy,
every time-management lapse.
He was brilliant, but
he put us on edge.
A stiffness came over the office.
"Sudhir's coming! Sudhir's coming!"
we'd whisper and we'd buckle down.
No one was particularly nice to Sudhir.
He made us anxious, so we resented him.

But one night I had a dream of Sudhir Singh Gupta.
In the dream, he wore a turban with an
emerald and ruby serpech.
And nothing else.
We lay together in a bed of crimson silks
under a canopy decorated with silver schrooms.
He was so gently passionate.
We made love like 1001 Nights.

After that night, that dream,
I felt at ease with him.
I smiled at him.

This Indian man, intense as a sapper,
smiled back.
After some time, we even laughed
with one another.
A dream caused this conversion.

When Sudhir Singh Gupta's consultancy was over,
on leaving, he gave to me a green enameled box.
Inside—written in the painterly Bengali script—
Tagore's beautiful poem about fireflies,
pansies, pearl shells, love and dreams.

A Single Man

The man and I were close.
Simpatico.
Confidantes.
Sympathizers.
He lived in another state,
so we rarely saw one another.
But we talked frequently over the phone.
It was like this over some years.
He was lonely.
I was the one friend.

One night he made the three-hour drive
to my town.
We went to a nice restaurant
by the seawall.
We drank wine, we laughed,
we shared even more secrets.
Later, we bedded.
It was inevitable.

Afterwards, lying in the dark
in each other's arms,
I said to him, "I love you."
And it was true.

"Oh," he said to the darkness,
to the winter night, to the universe,
"I don't think I love anybody."

Such a lonely man.

Id Est

In grade school, we were taught by the priest
we should choose to be murdered
like St. Maria Goretti (how he loved her!)
rather than give up our purity.
He said we'd live forever then,
married to God.

In high school, it was told by boys
that they could tell a girl was not a virgin
by the way she walked.

When I was in college, a football player told me
a frigid woman is a deformed woman—
her yoni is a snake's head.

And later, my first lover,
a Manhattan personal injury lawyer,
told me he could smell
when a woman had her period.

Myth is more powerful than truth.
Myth is wild and so unbelievable
we long to believe it. Myth speaks
to the id, which craves more
wildness than the mind wants fact.

And so I was a young girl constantly
questioning if I could die for my virginity,
then a teen with a self-conscious walk,

then a young woman longing to be deflowered—
not out of love, but as proof I was not frigid.
The young woman I became
fumigated herself with English Lavender
and avoided all males
when she was menstruating.

So I ask now—you boys, you men—
is there anything I can do for you today
that will mitigate your insecurities,
alleviate your ignorance,
moderate your arrogance,
dim your id?

One Man's Meat

for my ex

When he told her he wanted a divorce,
he said, by way of explanation,
"We don't fill each other's needs."
Shot through the heart,
she could only bleat, "What needs?"
Sitting in his big green chair,
feet propped up, ashtray on his lap,
he took a long drag.
He breathed out.
He turned.
His large head swung in blue smoke
like a ham in a smokehouse.
He spoke.
"I've asked you twice to buy Hamburger Helper,
and you never did."

Oh, Hamburger Helper!
The very glue of marriage!
The very spice! The greatest aphrodisiac!
Oh, helper of hamburger,
oh minced parsley, dried garlic,
potassium sulfate and celery seeds!
Oh, husband, she did not fill your needs!

Soldiering On

I had a lover, an ex-marine,
who, though he was older,
held himself tall, was clean-cut,
polite and high-minded.
Before we would bed,
he'd brush his teeth, fold his clothes,
set up the grey Zenith record player
and stack up his old 33's.
He loved music when he made love.

But the music he loved was march music.
It was *Grand March* from *Aida*.
It was *War March of the Priests*.
It was *March of the Toreadors*,
And it was Sousa, Sousa, Sousa.

Parade sex,
military love,
all drums and cymbals.
His body moved like a regiment.
His eyes shone like jackboots.
It was war.

At first, I tiptoed around,
as women do,
trying to accede to his needs.
But when sex became drill,
I asked if we could love
without marching.
He looked sad.

He said simply,
"I cannot."

We all dance to the music of time,
but he marched to a different drummer.
In the end, we had to accept
we were out of step.

Mal

He'd been though some things.
That first night after making love
he'd asked hopefully,
"Am I home, momma?"
A child's question.
From a man.

After that, he didn't ask
if he were home
or call me momma.
What he said was, "I love you,"
and moved in.

We set up a life.
It was good.
Except for the times, without warning,
when he'd jump up from the bed, the couch,
his chair, to cry, "Somethin' ain't right!"
waving his hands as if hornets were swarming the room.
He'd walk around and around in a deep fear,
unable to tell me what it was that wasn't right.
Then he'd begin shouting, "Back! Get back!"
swinging and stabbing at the murderous air.
In the end, he'd take himself away,
leaving in a panic by the back door.

He'd always come back, though, two or three days later,
the demons following, but silent.
And so it was that the demons came to live with us.
I thought my love could drive them away

or, if not, I could learn to live with them, too.
But something wasn't right.
Every several days the demons would wake
and strike.
It was like watching a repetitive slaughter—
the butchering of a spirit.
In the end, to save myself,
I had to send him away.

And nothing is right.

Stratford Morning

Six a.m.
Small birds dithering in the wisteria,
drinking blue fog and breathing blossom.
Cocking their heads from side to side,
they spy with one black eye then the other.

The coffee steams.
The ticking clock marks silence.
No phone has rung.
No letter's been delivered.
No one's been betrayed or
       said a cruel thing.
Nothing yet's been broken, lost, or made.

There's just the blue-fogged
virgin morning
and the small voice that
habitually sings in my blood:
       Perhaps today is the day
       I come to a corner,
       turn it
       and meet someone to love.

VI. HOW YOU SAY...?

One of Those Days

The morning sky is china white,
the clouds dark blue—a negative of normal.
I watch a pointy-headed possum,
supposed to be nocturnal,
wade through the dew and the grass.
I pour hot tea into my mug—it shatters
like a cherry bomb.
The postman comes at noon instead of nine.
And when the sun is at its height,
it briefly rains from brilliant skies—
and only in my yard.

The day is strange and getting stranger.
There could be lions in the streets.
I am low-key excited, I am leery,
I am curious and cheery,
I'm in an expectant state of mind.
In this psychological condition,
I grow alert to the entirety—
I hear the roses, smell the crickets,
see banana trees that aren't there.

My cells are super-sensitized,
my eyeballs have been husked.
I've been deskinned.
Words sing within,
and words will out.
I'll make another cup of tea,
perhaps another after that.
For it's a good day, a very good day
for poetry.

Hinky Dinky Parlez Vous

The Eskimo word for "love"
is also the word for "laugh."
The Latin word for "love"
is also the word for "bitter."
And so I imagine
—I have not looked it up—
that "love" could also mean,
say in Tanzania, "clay pot,"
or in Saudi Arabia, "money,"
or in Newfoundland, "warm dog."
"Love" might, in beautiful Hawaii,
also mean pineapple or Conger eel.

Think of all the countries in the world
in which the word for love might have
a double meaning.
Truth to tell, love itself can be
a many-meaninged thing—
depending on how you choose
to interpret it.

"Words, words, words," says Hamlet
to befuddle Polonius.
And words do befuddle.
So be careful in what language,
be cautious with what words you choose,
to tell your lover that you love her.
And mean it when you say it,
to a mafioso particularly,
or you may die "la petite mort"
literally.

Very Small and All Good

She was a lady poet.
Like the miniature landscapes
on ceramic broaches sold at the church fair,
her poems were small.
The subject of her poems was always nature—
the sunset all pinky-pink, a golden butterfly,
a pale moon over waves. Clichés.
Never did she write of love or sex or death,
or have a genuine thought.

Like her poems, her demeanor was exceptionally precise.
She stood straight as a caryatid at the lectern.
Her grammar was spectacularly correct,
and she wrote in indelible ink with a proper fountain pen.
She sprinkled her poems with French,
always quoted a venerable Greek or two,
knew to clinch each poem with some
obiter dictum of Audubon or Linnaeus.

These very, very sincere poems of hers showed schooling.
She knew arcane words to describe the bees and birds.
But she used no words at all to illuminate mankind's
feelings, ideas, philosophies or deeds.
And like those painted broaches at the fair,
her poems did never sell
except to very good old ladies who dreamt of heaven
but never would acknowledge hell.

Death, You Bitch

I visited my dying friend.
She was white white white and her bones
looked sprung, they were so sharp.
She opened her eyes to look at me only a few times.
I talked about my cat—she always loved cats.
I talked about the wisteria growing crazy all over my yard.
I talked about my new curtains—sheer—
how they let the light in.
None of this could a dying person care about.
I talked so she could hear a human voice.

When her eyes stayed closed for a very long time,
I tip-toed to the door.
I turned for a last look
and saw her eyes were open
and watching me intensely—
eyes so black and shining, they looked
like the eyes of a zealot,
a political prisoner,
a reformer,
a lover.
It must have taken all her strength to look at me like that.
What I said to her then was,
"Courage, Bonnie."
And, so very weakly, she held up her thumb as if to say,
"I've got this. I'll be brave. You can count on me."

Bonnie died that evening.
Since then I've thought on how unfeeling,
what school-teacher morality,

what drill-master instruction for heroics
I'd demanded of my dying friend.
Courage? *Courage?*
I should have said to her,
Weep, Bonnie! Weep for your life.
Go ahead, be my guest.
Grieve loud, grieve all you want, my friend.
Curse, cry, rage against your dying.
Death is the bitch who will murder you.
Accuse! Accuse!

The Tunnel

He had sorrows and afflictions
more than anyone should have to bear.
After I'd been told he took his life,
I remembered his last call.
He was in a dark, dark place, so I told him
all those weasel words—
all those unforgivable clichés we say
when we're not paying close attention,
or when we lack the experience to recognize
or the imagination to see
the depth, the danger, of another's darkness.

I gave my sales pitch.
I told him things would get better.
I said it's always darkest before dawn.
I gave him dreck he could not hear,
it was so dark in his head—
and they were lies.
Then I said—yes, I said this—
"There's light at the end of the tunnel."
And I remember.
I remember that he said,
"The tunnel is too long."

Pen & Ink

Always on the road, my father
would come home almost a stranger.
Like Ulysses, only more thoughtful—
he always returned bearing gifts.
Ragged from driving a thousand miles
straight through, he'd carry in his gifts for us,
watch us open them,
then sleep for two days.

The gifts he brought were from the Rexalls,
the LaVerdieres, the small drugstores along the way
where he'd stop for his Old Golds and coffee.
At the counter where amber apothecary bottles
and the brilliant show globes glowed,
he'd choose Coty's Dusting Power for my mother.
For my little brother, "The Green Lantern" comics,
Matchbox cars, and candy cigarettes.
A Kewpie doll or *Little Lady Toilet Water* for me.

But once I turned nine, it was always pens.
Fountain pens in satin-lined boxes—
silver Sheaffers, black and gold Watermans,
Parkers, Crosses—
pens good to hold, solid and serious.
Writing tools so sleek and beautiful, they inspired me
to write my copy-cat Nancy Drew stories,
perfect the Palmer Method in my diary,
write pen-pal letters to pals I didn't know
just to watch the black-inked words
glaze the page.

To me, my father was as mysterious as God.
But unlike God, he never laid guilt
nor dealt out instruction.
He simply gave his gifts of pens to me,
divining me somehow,
counseling me in a silent, slanted way:
Write.

The Elderly Thought Fox

after Ted Hughes

He comes, he comes—am I imagining?—
the little gold fox in the nighttime.
He's crossing the meadow daintily
in his black stockinged feet—
so delicately it seems he is trotting on air.
I see him. I don't see him.

The old and moldy moon
sheds a dull light on this page
my pen idles over.
The fox hesitates. He listens.
His black ears pivot like radar.
His black nose lifts to a scent.

I see him by snatches
coming through the high sweetgrass,
tail-tip a white flag that lifts
and drops in the wind.
Just there! I can see his eyes now—
yellow and glowing.
He sees mine.
And he hops straight up like a jackrabbit,
spins midair, and is gone.

My mind is empty.
I can't remember what it is
I was hoping he'd bring me.
And I can't recall…what *is* that word?

(I hunt the word *evanesced*,
but it stays hid in my brambled brain.)
Well, anyway, I'll just say it:
the fox has vanished.

There must be a hole in my head
through which the fox escaped.
The old moon shuffles through the clouds.
The page is blank.

VII. COLORS

In Florida

Winters, in the late 1940's and early 50's,
my father raced horses at Hialeah.
My mother would make the long drive
from Rhode Island to Florida in our two-toned DeSoto
so we could be with him for the racetrack season.
My younger brother and I sat in the backseat
stupefied with boredom.
It was a long, long drive.
The telephone poles stretched out forever on old Route 1,
marking monotony like a silent metronome.
Road signs were the only entertainment—

> Within this vale
> Of toil and sin
> Your head goes bald
> But not your chin.
> BURMA-SHAVE

WATCH FOR BOARS

BRYLCREEM—"A Little Dab'll Do Ya!"

PANTHER Xing

Five miles to Stucky's —-"Hey America...come on by!"

SINKHOLES

I remember driving through Georgia
early dawn, ours the only car on the road.

So cold.
I remember seeing black children
standing barefoot on frost next to a sign:
      PECANS 4 SALE
But where were their shoes?
But why weren't they in school?
Pickaninnies, my mother called them.
(I had never seen black skin before,
except for Little Black Sambo and that Tar Baby.
But they weren't real.)
They were calling out to us, "Pecans! Pecans!"
holding up their baskets, running barefoot after us
across the frosted, stubbled field.
We never stopped.

One warm evening in Tampa,
my parents' friends took us for a ride
through a settlement outside of town
to see how the darkies lived.
Eeny meeny miny moe.
Oaks swagged with moss shaded grey shacks.
We gaped at the black folks sitting on their porches.
Dusty chickens, skinny dogs.
The friend's big white Pontiac drove 10 miles an hour
down dirt lanes narrow as church aisles
while we gawked.
Singing coming from somewhere.
And my mother, a truly good and kind woman,
shaking her head sadly, saying,
 "Lazy. Lazy. They say they stay up all night
singing and dancing, so they're too tired
to work in the daytime."
Eeny meeny miny moe.

We visited a Seminole village.
My Auntie bought me a Seminole doll,
her tribal dress layers and layers of colors.
We watched Seminole women sew these dolls
on treadle sewing machines small as toys.
We watched a Seminole man wrestle a sluggish alligator.
He put it to sleep by rubbing sand on its belly.
What wonders!   What new world!
Then Auntie approached a Seminole lady
sitting sewing under her palm-thatched hut.
Auntie asked, "What do your *men* do around here?"
Like the police.
The woman did not raise her eyes from her sewing.
She kept her head bent low.
She did not answer.
And Auntie, a generous woman who had just
bought me a Seminole doll, curled her lip.
"Look at her!" she sneered. "She understands
what I'm saying. She's *ignoring* us!"
her breath labored with outrage.

Once I was taken to the racetrack's backstretch
to see the horses being shod.
I watched, fascinated, until the farrier at his red-hot forge
winked at me and drawled, "Little girl, do you know why
there aren't any Negro jockeys?"
I shook my head.
"Because," he said, "the horses can't stand the smell!"
And he made a sound like a coffee percolator,
only it was his kind of laugh.
I looked around and saw black men grooming the horses,
sudsing them up, brushing them down, stroking their noses,
pressing their faces to the horses' muzzles.

And the horses seemed to like that.
I was silent because I was nine
and it was a grownup telling me this.

In school, the Cuban kids were called "Cubes."
Like a thrown stone.
In school, I was called "Yankee."
Like a thrown stone.
In school, a teacher whispered to another,
"Race track trash," while I stood before them
in line, duteous as a postulant.

In school, the Cuban girls were so exotic!
They stood apart chattering in Spanish.
Their colorful skirts, their
curly hair piled up on their heads.
And jewels in the holes in their ears!
I yearned to know them.
But, "Stay away from them!" from Auntie.
"They're colored!"
I longed to touch their hair.

In those years when I was a child,
I had never heard the word "prejudice" or "racist."
I didn't know one Negro or one Seminole.
I didn't know one Arab, one Chinese, one Jew.
I didn't know anything.
I only knew Florida—its royal palms and
sparkling waters, the bluish Spanish moss,
those white magnolias, the red hibiscus.
I only knew a puzzling sadness growing in me,
vague but persistent and pernicious as kudzu,
a bewildering sorrow, ungraspable,

a greying-over of my spirit.

Oh God, Florida, your flowers!
The colors of your flowers!

ABOUT THE AUTHOR

Norah Pollard is a backwater poet with an oceanfront view of the world. She has published five collections of poetry, most recently *Lizard Season* (2018) and *In Deep* (2012). She lives in Stratford, Connecticut, very, very quietly.

This book is set in Garamond. During the mid-fifteen hundreds, Claude Garamond—a Parisian punch-cutter—produced a refined array of book types that combined an unprecedented degree of balance and elegance, for centuries standing as the pinnacle of beauty and practicality in type-founding.

For more concerning the work of Norah Pollard, visit www.antrimhousebooks.com/authors.html.
This book is available at all bookstores including Amazon.

www.ingramcontent.com/pod-product-compliance
Lightning Source LLC
Chambersburg PA
CBHW030154100526
44592CB00009B/275